50 Baked Bread Favorites Recipes for Home

By: Kelly Johnson

Table of Contents

- Classic French Baguette
- Whole Wheat Sandwich Bread
- Soft Dinner Rolls
- Sourdough Bread
- Cinnamon Raisin Bread
- Italian Focaccia
- Buttermilk Biscuits
- Challah Bread
- Garlic Herb Artisan Bread
- Irish Soda Bread
- Multigrain Bread
- Brioche Loaf
- Honey Oat Bread
- Cheddar Jalapeño Bread
- Rye Bread
- Parmesan Herb Breadsticks
- Lemon Poppy Seed Bread
- Sweet Potato Bread
- Pumpkin Bread
- Zucchini Bread
- Blueberry Muffin Bread
- Pretzel Rolls
- Whole Wheat Flatbread
- Caramelized Onion Bread
- Rustic Italian Bread
- Fluffy White Bread
- Spelt Bread
- Sun-Dried Tomato Basil Bread
- Almond Apricot Bread
- Sweet Cinnamon Pull-Apart Bread
- Pita Bread
- Rosemary Olive Oil Bread
- Chocolate Chip Banana Bread
- Apple Cinnamon Bread
- Beer Bread

- Sesame Seed Bread
- Greek Yogurt Honey Bread
- Potato Bread
- Maple Oatmeal Bread
- Cranberry Walnut Bread
- Country Rye Bread
- Fig and Walnut Bread
- Soft Pretzels
- Asiago Cheese Bread
- Muesli Bread
- Apple Cheddar Bread
- Sweet Cornbread
- Coconut Flour Bread
- Herb and Cheese Scones
- Stuffed Garlic Bread

Classic French Baguette

Ingredients:

- 3 1/2 cups all-purpose flour
- 1 1/2 cups warm water
- 2 tsp active dry yeast
- 1 1/2 tsp salt
- 1 tsp sugar

Instructions:

1. **Activate Yeast:** In a small bowl, dissolve sugar in warm water. Sprinkle yeast over the top and let sit for 5-10 minutes until frothy.
2. **Prepare Dough:** In a large bowl, mix flour and salt. Add yeast mixture and stir until dough forms.
3. **Knead and Rise:** Turn dough onto a floured surface and knead for 10 minutes until smooth. Place in a greased bowl, cover with a damp cloth, and let rise in a warm place for 1-1.5 hours, or until doubled in size.
4. **Shape Baguettes:** Punch down dough and divide into 2-3 equal pieces. Shape each piece into a long, thin loaf. Place on a parchment-lined baking sheet and let rise for 30 minutes.
5. **Bake:** Preheat oven to 475°F (245°C). Slash the tops of the loaves with a sharp knife. Bake for 20-25 minutes, or until golden brown and hollow sounding when tapped. Cool on a wire rack.

Whole Wheat Sandwich Bread

Ingredients:

- 2 cups whole wheat flour
- 1 cup all-purpose flour
- 1 1/2 cups warm water
- 2 tbsp honey
- 2 tsp active dry yeast
- 1/4 cup olive oil
- 1 1/2 tsp salt

Instructions:

1. **Activate Yeast:** In a bowl, dissolve honey in warm water. Sprinkle yeast over the top and let sit for 5-10 minutes until frothy.
2. **Prepare Dough:** In a large bowl, mix whole wheat flour, all-purpose flour, and salt. Add yeast mixture and olive oil. Stir until dough forms.
3. **Knead and Rise:** Turn dough onto a floured surface and knead for 8-10 minutes until smooth. Place in a greased bowl, cover, and let rise for 1 hour, or until doubled in size.
4. **Shape and Bake:** Punch down dough and shape into a loaf. Place in a greased loaf pan and let rise for 30 minutes. Preheat oven to 375°F (190°C) and bake for 30-35 minutes, or until the top is golden and the loaf sounds hollow when tapped. Cool on a wire rack.

Soft Dinner Rolls

Ingredients:

- 3 1/2 cups all-purpose flour
- 1 cup warm milk
- 1/4 cup sugar
- 1/4 cup butter, melted
- 2 tsp active dry yeast
- 1/2 tsp salt
- 1 large egg

Instructions:

1. **Activate Yeast:** In a bowl, dissolve sugar in warm milk. Sprinkle yeast over the top and let sit for 5-10 minutes until frothy.
2. **Prepare Dough:** In a large bowl, mix flour and salt. Add yeast mixture, melted butter, and egg. Stir until dough forms.
3. **Knead and Rise:** Turn dough onto a floured surface and knead for 8 minutes until smooth. Place in a greased bowl, cover, and let rise for 1 hour, or until doubled in size.
4. **Shape Rolls:** Punch down dough and divide into 12 equal pieces. Shape into balls and place in a greased baking dish. Let rise for 30 minutes.
5. **Bake:** Preheat oven to 375°F (190°C). Bake rolls for 15-20 minutes, or until golden brown. Cool on a wire rack.

Sourdough Bread

Ingredients:

- 1 cup active sourdough starter
- 1 1/2 cups warm water
- 4 cups all-purpose flour
- 2 tsp salt

Instructions:

1. **Mix Dough:** In a large bowl, combine sourdough starter, warm water, and 2 cups of flour. Stir until smooth. Gradually add remaining flour and salt. Stir until dough forms.
2. **Knead and Rise:** Turn dough onto a floured surface and knead for 10 minutes until smooth. Place in a greased bowl, cover, and let rise for 1-2 hours, or until doubled in size.
3. **Shape and Rise:** Punch down dough and shape into a loaf. Place in a greased loaf pan and let rise for 30-60 minutes.
4. **Bake:** Preheat oven to 450°F (230°C). Bake for 30-35 minutes, or until golden brown and hollow sounding when tapped. Cool on a wire rack.

Cinnamon Raisin Bread

Ingredients:

- 3 1/2 cups all-purpose flour
- 1 cup milk
- 1/2 cup sugar
- 1/4 cup butter, softened
- 2 tsp active dry yeast
- 1/2 tsp salt
- 1 cup raisins
- 2 tbsp ground cinnamon

Instructions:

1. **Activate Yeast:** In a bowl, dissolve sugar in warm milk. Sprinkle yeast over the top and let sit for 5-10 minutes until frothy.
2. **Prepare Dough:** In a large bowl, mix flour and salt. Add yeast mixture and softened butter. Stir until dough forms.
3. **Knead and Rise:** Turn dough onto a floured surface and knead for 8-10 minutes until smooth. Add raisins and cinnamon while kneading. Place in a greased bowl, cover, and let rise for 1 hour.
4. **Shape and Bake:** Punch down dough and shape into a loaf. Place in a greased loaf pan and let rise for 30 minutes. Preheat oven to 375°F (190°C) and bake for 30-35 minutes, or until golden brown and hollow sounding when tapped. Cool on a wire rack.

Italian Focaccia

Ingredients:

- 3 1/2 cups all-purpose flour
- 1 1/2 cups warm water
- 1/4 cup olive oil
- 2 tsp active dry yeast
- 1 tbsp fresh rosemary, chopped
- 2 tsp salt
- Coarse sea salt for sprinkling

Instructions:

1. **Activate Yeast:** In a bowl, dissolve yeast in warm water. Let sit for 5-10 minutes until frothy.
2. **Prepare Dough:** In a large bowl, mix flour and salt. Add yeast mixture and olive oil. Stir until dough forms.
3. **Knead and Rise:** Turn dough onto a floured surface and knead for 5-6 minutes. Place in a greased bowl, cover, and let rise for 1 hour.
4. **Shape and Bake:** Punch down dough and transfer to a greased baking sheet. Press dough into a rectangle and make dimples with your fingers. Sprinkle with rosemary and coarse sea salt. Let rise for 30 minutes. Preheat oven to 425°F (220°C) and bake for 20-25 minutes, or until golden brown. Cool on a wire rack.

Buttermilk Biscuits

Ingredients:

- 2 cups all-purpose flour
- 1/4 cup cold butter, cubed
- 1 tbsp baking powder
- 1/2 tsp baking soda
- 1/2 tsp salt
- 3/4 cup buttermilk

Instructions:

1. **Prepare Dough:** In a bowl, mix flour, baking powder, baking soda, and salt. Cut in butter until the mixture resembles coarse crumbs. Stir in buttermilk until just combined.
2. **Roll and Cut:** Turn dough onto a floured surface and roll to about 1-inch thickness. Cut out biscuits with a round cutter.
3. **Bake:** Place biscuits on a baking sheet and bake at 425°F (220°C) for 12-15 minutes, or until golden brown. Cool on a wire rack.

Challah Bread

Ingredients:

- 4 cups all-purpose flour
- 1 cup warm water
- 1/2 cup sugar
- 1/4 cup vegetable oil
- 2 large eggs
- 2 tsp active dry yeast
- 1 tsp salt
- 1 egg (for egg wash)

Instructions:

1. **Activate Yeast:** Dissolve sugar in warm water. Sprinkle yeast over the top and let sit for 5-10 minutes until frothy.
2. **Prepare Dough:** In a large bowl, mix flour and salt. Add yeast mixture, oil, and eggs. Stir until dough forms.
3. **Knead and Rise:** Turn dough onto a floured surface and knead for 8-10 minutes until smooth. Place in a greased bowl, cover, and let rise for 1-2 hours, or until doubled in size.
4. **Shape and Bake:** Punch down dough and divide into 3 equal pieces. Braid the pieces and place on a greased baking sheet. Let rise for 30 minutes. Preheat oven to 375°F (190°C). Brush with egg wash and bake for 25-30 minutes, or until golden brown. Cool on a wire rack.

Garlic Herb Artisan Bread

Ingredients:

- 3 cups all-purpose flour
- 1 1/2 cups warm water
- 1 tbsp olive oil
- 1 tsp salt
- 1 tsp sugar
- 2 tsp active dry yeast
- 3 cloves garlic, minced
- 2 tbsp fresh parsley, chopped
- 1 tbsp fresh rosemary, chopped

Instructions:

1. **Activate Yeast:** In a small bowl, dissolve sugar in warm water. Sprinkle yeast over the top and let sit for 5-10 minutes until frothy.
2. **Prepare Dough:** In a large bowl, mix flour, salt, garlic, parsley, and rosemary. Add yeast mixture and olive oil. Stir until dough forms.
3. **Knead and Rise:** Turn dough onto a floured surface and knead for 8-10 minutes until smooth. Place in a greased bowl, cover, and let rise for 1-2 hours, or until doubled in size.
4. **Shape and Bake:** Punch down dough and shape into a round loaf. Place on a parchment-lined baking sheet. Let rise for 30 minutes. Preheat oven to 450°F (230°C) and bake for 25-30 minutes, or until golden brown and hollow sounding when tapped. Cool on a wire rack.

Irish Soda Bread

Ingredients:

- 4 cups all-purpose flour
- 1/4 cup sugar
- 1 tsp baking soda
- 1/2 tsp baking powder
- 1/2 tsp salt
- 1/2 cup cold butter, cubed
- 1 1/2 cups buttermilk
- 1 large egg
- 1 cup raisins (optional)

Instructions:

1. **Prepare Dough:** In a large bowl, mix flour, sugar, baking soda, baking powder, and salt. Cut in butter until the mixture resembles coarse crumbs. Stir in buttermilk and egg until just combined. Fold in raisins if using.
2. **Shape and Bake:** Transfer dough to a floured surface and shape into a round loaf. Place on a greased baking sheet or in a cast-iron skillet. Cut a deep cross in the top of the loaf. Bake at 375°F (190°C) for 35-40 minutes, or until golden brown and a toothpick inserted in the center comes out clean. Cool on a wire rack.

Multigrain Bread

Ingredients:

- 2 cups whole wheat flour
- 1 cup all-purpose flour
- 1/2 cup rolled oats
- 1/4 cup flaxseeds
- 1/4 cup sunflower seeds
- 1/4 cup honey
- 1 1/2 cups warm water
- 2 tsp active dry yeast
- 1/4 cup olive oil
- 1 1/2 tsp salt

Instructions:

1. **Activate Yeast:** In a small bowl, dissolve honey in warm water. Sprinkle yeast over the top and let sit for 5-10 minutes until frothy.
2. **Prepare Dough:** In a large bowl, mix whole wheat flour, all-purpose flour, oats, flaxseeds, sunflower seeds, and salt. Add yeast mixture and olive oil. Stir until dough forms.
3. **Knead and Rise:** Turn dough onto a floured surface and knead for 8-10 minutes until smooth. Place in a greased bowl, cover, and let rise for 1-2 hours, or until doubled in size.
4. **Shape and Bake:** Punch down dough and shape into a loaf. Place in a greased loaf pan and let rise for 30 minutes. Preheat oven to 375°F (190°C) and bake for 35-40 minutes, or until golden brown and hollow sounding when tapped. Cool on a wire rack.

Brioche Loaf

Ingredients:

- 3 1/2 cups all-purpose flour
- 1/2 cup sugar
- 1 cup warm milk
- 1/2 cup unsalted butter, softened
- 4 large eggs
- 2 tsp active dry yeast
- 1/2 tsp salt

Instructions:

1. **Activate Yeast:** In a small bowl, dissolve sugar in warm milk. Sprinkle yeast over the top and let sit for 5-10 minutes until frothy.
2. **Prepare Dough:** In a large bowl, mix flour and salt. Add yeast mixture, softened butter, and eggs. Stir until dough forms.
3. **Knead and Rise:** Turn dough onto a floured surface and knead for 8-10 minutes until smooth. Place in a greased bowl, cover, and let rise for 1-2 hours, or until doubled in size.
4. **Shape and Bake:** Punch down dough and shape into a loaf. Place in a greased loaf pan and let rise for 30-60 minutes. Preheat oven to 375°F (190°C) and bake for 30-35 minutes, or until golden brown and a toothpick inserted in the center comes out clean. Cool on a wire rack.

Honey Oat Bread

Ingredients:

- 2 cups whole wheat flour
- 1 cup all-purpose flour
- 1 cup rolled oats
- 1/4 cup honey
- 1 1/2 cups warm water
- 2 tsp active dry yeast
- 1/4 cup olive oil
- 1 1/2 tsp salt

Instructions:

1. **Activate Yeast:** In a small bowl, dissolve honey in warm water. Sprinkle yeast over the top and let sit for 5-10 minutes until frothy.
2. **Prepare Dough:** In a large bowl, mix whole wheat flour, all-purpose flour, oats, and salt. Add yeast mixture and olive oil. Stir until dough forms.
3. **Knead and Rise:** Turn dough onto a floured surface and knead for 8-10 minutes until smooth. Place in a greased bowl, cover, and let rise for 1-2 hours, or until doubled in size.
4. **Shape and Bake:** Punch down dough and shape into a loaf. Place in a greased loaf pan and let rise for 30 minutes. Preheat oven to 375°F (190°C) and bake for 30-35 minutes, or until golden brown and hollow sounding when tapped. Cool on a wire rack.

Cheddar Jalapeño Bread

Ingredients:

- 3 cups all-purpose flour
- 1 1/2 cups shredded sharp cheddar cheese
- 2 jalapeños, finely chopped
- 1 cup warm milk
- 1/4 cup butter, softened
- 2 tsp active dry yeast
- 1 1/2 tsp salt
- 1 tbsp sugar

Instructions:

1. **Activate Yeast:** In a small bowl, dissolve sugar in warm milk. Sprinkle yeast over the top and let sit for 5-10 minutes until frothy.
2. **Prepare Dough:** In a large bowl, mix flour and salt. Add yeast mixture, softened butter, cheddar cheese, and jalapeños. Stir until dough forms.
3. **Knead and Rise:** Turn dough onto a floured surface and knead for 8-10 minutes until smooth. Place in a greased bowl, cover, and let rise for 1-2 hours, or until doubled in size.
4. **Shape and Bake:** Punch down dough and shape into a loaf. Place in a greased loaf pan and let rise for 30 minutes. Preheat oven to 375°F (190°C) and bake for 30-35 minutes, or until golden brown and a toothpick inserted in the center comes out clean. Cool on a wire rack.

Rye Bread

Ingredients:

- 2 cups rye flour
- 1 cup all-purpose flour
- 1 1/2 cups warm water
- 2 tbsp caraway seeds
- 1 tbsp molasses
- 2 tsp active dry yeast
- 1 1/2 tsp salt

Instructions:

1. **Activate Yeast:** In a small bowl, dissolve molasses in warm water. Sprinkle yeast over the top and let sit for 5-10 minutes until frothy.
2. **Prepare Dough:** In a large bowl, mix rye flour, all-purpose flour, caraway seeds, and salt. Add yeast mixture and stir until dough forms.
3. **Knead and Rise:** Turn dough onto a floured surface and knead for 8-10 minutes until smooth. Place in a greased bowl, cover, and let rise for 1-2 hours, or until doubled in size.
4. **Shape and Bake:** Punch down dough and shape into a loaf. Place in a greased loaf pan and let rise for 30 minutes. Preheat oven to 375°F (190°C) and bake for 35-40 minutes, or until golden brown and hollow sounding when tapped. Cool on a wire rack.

Parmesan Herb Breadsticks

Ingredients:

- 2 cups all-purpose flour
- 1/2 cup grated Parmesan cheese
- 1/4 cup olive oil
- 1 cup warm water
- 2 tsp active dry yeast
- 1 tsp dried basil
- 1 tsp dried oregano
- 1 tsp garlic powder
- 1/2 tsp salt

Instructions:

1. **Activate Yeast:** In a small bowl, dissolve yeast in warm water. Let sit for 5-10 minutes until frothy.
2. **Prepare Dough:** In a large bowl, mix flour, Parmesan cheese, basil, oregano, garlic powder, and salt. Add yeast mixture and olive oil. Stir until dough forms.
3. **Knead and Rise:** Turn dough onto a floured surface and knead for 5-6 minutes until smooth. Place in a greased bowl, cover, and let rise for 1 hour.
4. **Shape and Bake:** Punch down dough and roll out into a rectangle. Cut into sticks and place on a greased baking sheet. Bake at 375°F (190°C) for 15-20 minutes, or until golden brown. Cool on a wire rack.

Lemon Poppy Seed Bread

Ingredients:

- 1 1/2 cups all-purpose flour
- 1/2 cup sugar
- 1/2 cup unsalted butter, softened
- 2 large eggs
- 1/2 cup milk
- 2 tbsp lemon zest
- 2 tbsp lemon juice
- 1 tbsp poppy seeds
- 1 1/2 tsp baking powder
- 1/2 tsp baking soda
- 1/4 tsp salt

Instructions:

1. **Prepare Oven and Pan:** Preheat oven to 350°F (175°C). Grease and flour a loaf pan.
2. **Mix Ingredients:** In a medium bowl, whisk together flour, baking powder, baking soda, and salt. In another bowl, beat butter and sugar until creamy. Add eggs one at a time, mixing well after each. Stir in lemon zest, lemon juice, and milk. Gradually add dry ingredients, mixing just until combined. Fold in poppy seeds.
3. **Bake:** Pour batter into the prepared loaf pan. Bake for 50-60 minutes, or until a toothpick inserted in the center comes out clean. Cool in the pan for 10 minutes, then transfer to a wire rack to cool completely.

Sweet Potato Bread

Ingredients:

- 1 1/2 cups mashed sweet potatoes
- 1/2 cup sugar
- 1/2 cup brown sugar
- 1/2 cup vegetable oil
- 2 large eggs
- 1 1/2 cups all-purpose flour
- 1 tsp baking powder
- 1/2 tsp baking soda
- 1/2 tsp salt
- 1 tsp ground cinnamon
- 1/2 tsp ground nutmeg

Instructions:

1. **Prepare Oven and Pan:** Preheat oven to 350°F (175°C). Grease and flour a loaf pan.
2. **Mix Ingredients:** In a large bowl, mix sweet potatoes, sugar, brown sugar, and oil. Add eggs and mix well. In another bowl, whisk together flour, baking powder, baking soda, salt, cinnamon, and nutmeg. Gradually add dry ingredients to the sweet potato mixture, stirring until just combined.
3. **Bake:** Pour batter into the prepared loaf pan. Bake for 50-60 minutes, or until a toothpick inserted in the center comes out clean. Cool in the pan for 10 minutes, then transfer to a wire rack to cool completely.

Pumpkin Bread

Ingredients:

- 1 1/2 cups all-purpose flour
- 1 cup sugar
- 1/2 tsp baking powder
- 1/2 tsp baking soda
- 1/2 tsp salt
- 1 tsp ground cinnamon
- 1/2 tsp ground nutmeg
- 1/2 tsp ground cloves
- 1 cup canned pumpkin puree
- 1/2 cup vegetable oil
- 2 large eggs
- 1/4 cup water

Instructions:

1. **Prepare Oven and Pan:** Preheat oven to 350°F (175°C). Grease and flour a loaf pan.
2. **Mix Ingredients:** In a medium bowl, whisk together flour, sugar, baking powder, baking soda, salt, cinnamon, nutmeg, and cloves. In another bowl, mix pumpkin puree, oil, eggs, and water. Gradually add dry ingredients to the pumpkin mixture, stirring until just combined.
3. **Bake:** Pour batter into the prepared loaf pan. Bake for 60-70 minutes, or until a toothpick inserted in the center comes out clean. Cool in the pan for 10 minutes, then transfer to a wire rack to cool completely.

Zucchini Bread

Ingredients:

- 1 1/2 cups all-purpose flour
- 1/2 tsp baking powder
- 1/2 tsp baking soda
- 1/2 tsp salt
- 1 tsp ground cinnamon
- 1/2 cup sugar
- 1/2 cup brown sugar
- 1/2 cup vegetable oil
- 2 large eggs
- 1 cup grated zucchini (with moisture squeezed out)
- 1/2 cup chopped walnuts or pecans (optional)

Instructions:

1. **Prepare Oven and Pan:** Preheat oven to 350°F (175°C). Grease and flour a loaf pan.
2. **Mix Ingredients:** In a medium bowl, whisk together flour, baking powder, baking soda, salt, and cinnamon. In another bowl, beat sugars and oil until well blended. Add eggs one at a time, mixing well after each. Stir in grated zucchini. Gradually add dry ingredients, mixing until just combined. Fold in nuts if using.
3. **Bake:** Pour batter into the prepared loaf pan. Bake for 50-60 minutes, or until a toothpick inserted in the center comes out clean. Cool in the pan for 10 minutes, then transfer to a wire rack to cool completely.

Blueberry Muffin Bread

Ingredients:

- 1 1/2 cups all-purpose flour
- 1/2 cup sugar
- 1/2 tsp baking powder
- 1/2 tsp baking soda
- 1/4 tsp salt
- 1/2 cup unsalted butter, softened
- 1/4 cup milk
- 2 large eggs
- 1 cup fresh or frozen blueberries
- 1 tsp lemon zest (optional)

Instructions:

1. **Prepare Oven and Pan:** Preheat oven to 350°F (175°C). Grease and flour a loaf pan.
2. **Mix Ingredients:** In a medium bowl, whisk together flour, baking powder, baking soda, and salt. In another bowl, cream butter and sugar until light and fluffy. Beat in eggs one at a time. Gradually add flour mixture, alternating with milk, mixing just until combined. Gently fold in blueberries and lemon zest if using.
3. **Bake:** Pour batter into the prepared loaf pan. Bake for 55-65 minutes, or until a toothpick inserted in the center comes out clean. Cool in the pan for 10 minutes, then transfer to a wire rack to cool completely.

Pretzel Rolls

Ingredients:

- 1 1/2 cups warm water
- 1 packet (2 1/4 tsp) active dry yeast
- 1/4 cup granulated sugar
- 4 cups all-purpose flour
- 1 tsp salt
- 1/4 cup baking soda
- 1 large egg, beaten
- Coarse sea salt, for sprinkling

Instructions:

1. **Prepare Dough:** In a large bowl, dissolve yeast and sugar in warm water. Let sit for 5 minutes until frothy. Stir in flour and salt until a dough forms. Knead on a floured surface for 5-7 minutes, until smooth. Place in a lightly oiled bowl, cover, and let rise in a warm place for 1 hour or until doubled in size.
2. **Shape and Boil:** Preheat oven to 425°F (220°C). Punch down dough and divide into 12 pieces. Shape each piece into a ball and place on a baking sheet lined with parchment paper. In a large pot, bring 6 cups of water and baking soda to a boil. Boil pretzel rolls in batches for 30 seconds, then transfer to the baking sheet. Brush with beaten egg and sprinkle with coarse sea salt.
3. **Bake:** Bake for 12-15 minutes, or until golden brown. Cool on a wire rack.

Whole Wheat Flatbread

Ingredients:

- 1 1/2 cups whole wheat flour
- 1/2 cup all-purpose flour
- 1 tsp baking powder
- 1/2 tsp salt
- 1/2 cup plain yogurt
- 1/4 cup warm water
- 2 tbsp olive oil

Instructions:

1. **Prepare Dough:** In a bowl, mix whole wheat flour, all-purpose flour, baking powder, and salt. Stir in yogurt, warm water, and olive oil until a dough forms. Knead on a floured surface for a few minutes until smooth.
2. **Roll and Cook:** Divide dough into 4-6 pieces and roll each into a thin circle. Heat a skillet over medium-high heat. Cook each flatbread for 1-2 minutes on each side, or until lightly browned and cooked through. Serve warm.

Caramelized Onion Bread

Ingredients:

- 1 1/2 cups all-purpose flour
- 1/2 cup whole wheat flour
- 1 packet (2 1/4 tsp) active dry yeast
- 1/2 cup warm water
- 1/2 cup caramelized onions
- 1 tbsp sugar
- 1/2 tsp salt
- 1/4 cup olive oil

Instructions:

1. **Prepare Dough:** In a small bowl, dissolve yeast and sugar in warm water. Let sit for 5 minutes until frothy. In a large bowl, combine all-purpose flour, whole wheat flour, and salt. Stir in yeast mixture and olive oil until a dough forms. Knead on a floured surface for 5-7 minutes, until smooth.
2. **Add Onions and Rise:** Gently fold in caramelized onions. Place dough in a lightly oiled bowl, cover, and let rise in a warm place for 1 hour or until doubled in size.
3. **Bake:** Preheat oven to 375°F (190°C). Punch down dough and shape into a loaf. Place in a greased loaf pan and let rise for another 30 minutes. Bake for 30-35 minutes, or until golden brown and sounds hollow when tapped. Cool on a wire rack.

Rustic Italian Bread

Ingredients:

- 3 cups all-purpose flour
- 1 packet (2 1/4 tsp) active dry yeast
- 1 1/2 tsp salt
- 1 1/4 cups warm water
- 1 tbsp olive oil
- 1 tsp sugar

Instructions:

1. **Prepare Dough:** In a small bowl, dissolve yeast and sugar in warm water. Let sit for 5 minutes until frothy. In a large bowl, combine flour and salt. Stir in yeast mixture and olive oil until a dough forms. Knead on a floured surface for 8-10 minutes, until smooth.
2. **Rise and Shape:** Place dough in a lightly oiled bowl, cover, and let rise in a warm place for 1 hour or until doubled in size. Punch down dough and shape into a round loaf. Place on a parchment-lined baking sheet, cover, and let rise for another 30 minutes.
3. **Bake:** Preheat oven to 425°F (220°C). Bake for 25-30 minutes, or until the crust is golden and the bread sounds hollow when tapped. Cool on a wire rack.

Fluffy White Bread

Ingredients:

- 2 1/4 cups all-purpose flour
- 1 packet (2 1/4 tsp) active dry yeast
- 1/2 cup warm milk
- 1/4 cup granulated sugar
- 1/4 cup unsalted butter, softened
- 1/2 tsp salt
- 1 large egg

Instructions:

1. **Prepare Dough:** In a small bowl, dissolve yeast and sugar in warm milk. Let sit for 5 minutes until frothy. In a large bowl, combine flour and salt. Stir in yeast mixture, butter, and egg until a dough forms. Knead on a floured surface for 5-7 minutes, until smooth.
2. **Rise and Shape:** Place dough in a lightly oiled bowl, cover, and let rise in a warm place for 1 hour or until doubled in size. Punch down dough and shape into a loaf. Place in a greased loaf pan and let rise for another 30 minutes.
3. **Bake:** Preheat oven to 350°F (175°C). Bake for 30-35 minutes, or until golden brown and the bread sounds hollow when tapped. Cool on a wire rack.

Spelt Bread

Ingredients:

- 2 cups spelt flour
- 1 cup all-purpose flour
- 1 packet (2 1/4 tsp) active dry yeast
- 1 1/2 cups warm water
- 1 tbsp honey
- 1/4 cup olive oil
- 1 tsp salt

Instructions:

1. **Prepare Dough:** In a small bowl, dissolve yeast and honey in warm water. Let sit for 5 minutes until frothy. In a large bowl, combine spelt flour, all-purpose flour, and salt. Stir in yeast mixture and olive oil until a dough forms.
2. **Knead and Rise:** Knead dough on a floured surface for 8-10 minutes, until smooth. Place in a lightly oiled bowl, cover, and let rise in a warm place for 1 hour or until doubled in size.
3. **Shape and Bake:** Punch down dough and shape into a loaf. Place in a greased loaf pan and let rise for another 30 minutes. Preheat oven to 375°F (190°C). Bake for 30-35 minutes, or until golden brown and the bread sounds hollow when tapped. Cool on a wire rack.

Sun-Dried Tomato Basil Bread

Ingredients:

- 3 cups all-purpose flour
- 1 packet (2 1/4 tsp) active dry yeast
- 1 cup warm water
- 1/2 cup sun-dried tomatoes, chopped
- 1/4 cup fresh basil, chopped
- 2 tbsp olive oil
- 1 tsp sugar
- 1 tsp salt

Instructions:

1. **Prepare Dough:** In a small bowl, dissolve yeast and sugar in warm water. Let sit for 5 minutes until frothy. In a large bowl, combine flour and salt. Stir in yeast mixture, olive oil, sun-dried tomatoes, and basil until a dough forms.
2. **Knead and Rise:** Knead dough on a floured surface for 8-10 minutes, until smooth. Place in a lightly oiled bowl, cover, and let rise in a warm place for 1 hour or until doubled in size.
3. **Shape and Bake:** Punch down dough and shape into a loaf. Place in a greased loaf pan and let rise for another 30 minutes. Preheat oven to 375°F (190°C). Bake for 30-35 minutes, or until golden brown and the bread sounds hollow when tapped. Cool on a wire rack.

Almond Apricot Bread

Ingredients:

- 2 cups all-purpose flour
- 1/2 cup almond meal
- 1/2 cup dried apricots, chopped
- 1/2 cup sugar
- 1 packet (2 1/4 tsp) active dry yeast
- 1 cup warm milk
- 1/4 cup unsalted butter, softened
- 1/4 tsp salt

Instructions:

1. **Prepare Dough:** In a small bowl, dissolve yeast and sugar in warm milk. Let sit for 5 minutes until frothy. In a large bowl, combine flour, almond meal, and salt. Stir in yeast mixture and butter until a dough forms. Fold in chopped apricots.
2. **Knead and Rise:** Knead dough on a floured surface for 8-10 minutes, until smooth. Place in a lightly oiled bowl, cover, and let rise in a warm place for 1 hour or until doubled in size.
3. **Shape and Bake:** Punch down dough and shape into a loaf. Place in a greased loaf pan and let rise for another 30 minutes. Preheat oven to 350°F (175°C). Bake for 30-35 minutes, or until golden brown and the bread sounds hollow when tapped. Cool on a wire rack.

Sweet Cinnamon Pull-Apart Bread

Ingredients:

- 3 cups all-purpose flour
- 1 packet (2 1/4 tsp) active dry yeast
- 1/4 cup sugar
- 1/2 cup warm milk
- 1/4 cup unsalted butter, softened
- 1/2 tsp salt
- 1/2 cup brown sugar
- 2 tsp ground cinnamon

Instructions:

1. **Prepare Dough:** In a small bowl, dissolve yeast and sugar in warm milk. Let sit for 5 minutes until frothy. In a large bowl, combine flour, salt, and remaining sugar. Stir in yeast mixture and butter until a dough forms. Knead on a floured surface for 5-7 minutes, until smooth.
2. **Rise and Shape:** Place dough in a lightly oiled bowl, cover, and let rise in a warm place for 1 hour or until doubled in size. Punch down dough and roll out into a rectangle. Spread with melted butter, then sprinkle with brown sugar and cinnamon. Cut into strips, stack, and place in a greased loaf pan. Let rise for another 30 minutes.
3. **Bake:** Preheat oven to 350°F (175°C). Bake for 30-35 minutes, or until golden brown. Cool slightly before pulling apart.

Pita Bread

Ingredients:

- 2 cups all-purpose flour
- 1 cup whole wheat flour
- 1 packet (2 1/4 tsp) active dry yeast
- 1 1/2 cups warm water
- 1 tbsp olive oil
- 1 tsp salt
- 1 tsp sugar

Instructions:

1. **Prepare Dough:** In a small bowl, dissolve yeast and sugar in warm water. Let sit for 5 minutes until frothy. In a large bowl, combine flours and salt. Stir in yeast mixture and olive oil until a dough forms.
2. **Knead and Rise:** Knead dough on a floured surface for 5-7 minutes, until smooth. Place in a lightly oiled bowl, cover, and let rise in a warm place for 1 hour or until doubled in size.
3. **Shape and Bake:** Punch down dough and divide into 8-10 pieces. Roll each piece into a flat circle. Preheat oven to 475°F (245°C) and place a baking sheet or pizza stone inside. Bake pita rounds on the hot baking sheet for 5-7 minutes, or until puffy and lightly browned. Cool on a wire rack.

Rosemary Olive Oil Bread

Ingredients:

- 3 cups all-purpose flour
- 1 packet (2 1/4 tsp) active dry yeast
- 1 cup warm water
- 1/4 cup olive oil
- 2 tbsp fresh rosemary, chopped
- 1 tsp salt
- 1 tsp sugar

Instructions:

1. **Prepare Dough:** In a small bowl, dissolve yeast and sugar in warm water. Let sit for 5 minutes until frothy. In a large bowl, combine flour and salt. Stir in yeast mixture and olive oil until a dough forms. Add rosemary and mix well.
2. **Knead and Rise:** Knead dough on a floured surface for 8-10 minutes, until smooth. Place in a lightly oiled bowl, cover, and let rise in a warm place for 1 hour or until doubled in size.
3. **Shape and Bake:** Punch down dough and shape into a loaf. Place in a greased loaf pan and let rise for another 30 minutes. Preheat oven to 375°F (190°C). Bake for 30-35 minutes, or until golden brown and the bread sounds hollow when tapped. Cool on a wire rack.

Chocolate Chip Banana Bread

Ingredients:

- 1 1/2 cups all-purpose flour
- 1/2 cup sugar
- 1/4 cup brown sugar
- 1/2 tsp baking powder
- 1/2 tsp baking soda
- 1/4 tsp salt
- 1/2 cup butter, softened
- 2 large eggs
- 1 cup mashed ripe bananas (about 3 bananas)
- 1/2 cup chocolate chips

Instructions:

1. **Prepare Batter:** Preheat oven to 350°F (175°C). In a medium bowl, mix flour, sugar, brown sugar, baking powder, baking soda, and salt. In a separate bowl, cream butter and eggs until light and fluffy. Mix in bananas. Gradually add dry ingredients to the wet mixture, then fold in chocolate chips.
2. **Bake:** Pour batter into a greased loaf pan. Bake for 60-70 minutes, or until a toothpick inserted into the center comes out clean. Cool in the pan for 10 minutes before transferring to a wire rack to cool completely.

Apple Cinnamon Bread

Ingredients:

- 2 cups all-purpose flour
- 1/2 cup sugar
- 1/2 tsp baking powder
- 1/2 tsp baking soda
- 1/2 tsp salt
- 1 tsp ground cinnamon
- 1/2 cup unsalted butter, softened
- 1/2 cup brown sugar
- 2 large eggs
- 1 cup peeled and diced apples (about 1-2 apples)
- 1/4 cup milk

Instructions:

1. **Prepare Batter:** Preheat oven to 350°F (175°C). In a medium bowl, mix flour, sugar, baking powder, baking soda, salt, and cinnamon. In a separate bowl, cream butter and brown sugar until fluffy. Beat in eggs one at a time. Gradually add dry ingredients to the wet mixture, alternating with milk. Fold in diced apples.
2. **Bake:** Pour batter into a greased loaf pan. Bake for 50-60 minutes, or until a toothpick inserted into the center comes out clean. Cool in the pan for 10 minutes before transferring to a wire rack to cool completely.

Beer Bread

Ingredients:

- 3 cups all-purpose flour
- 1/4 cup sugar
- 1 tbsp baking powder

- 1/2 tsp salt
- 1 can (12 oz) beer (any kind)
- 1/4 cup melted butter

Instructions:

1. **Prepare Batter:** Preheat oven to 375°F (190°C). In a large bowl, mix flour, sugar, baking powder, and salt. Pour in beer and stir until just combined. The batter will be lumpy.
2. **Bake:** Pour batter into a greased loaf pan. Pour melted butter over the top of the batter. Bake for 50-60 minutes, or until golden brown and a toothpick inserted into the center comes out clean. Cool in the pan for 10 minutes before transferring to a wire rack to cool completely.

Sesame Seed Bread

Ingredients:

- 3 cups all-purpose flour
- 1 packet (2 1/4 tsp) active dry yeast
- 1 cup warm water
- 1/4 cup sesame seeds
- 2 tbsp olive oil
- 1 tsp salt
- 1 tsp sugar

Instructions:

1. **Prepare Dough:** In a small bowl, dissolve yeast and sugar in warm water. Let sit for 5 minutes until frothy. In a large bowl, combine flour and salt. Stir in yeast mixture and olive oil until a dough forms. Fold in sesame seeds.
2. **Knead and Rise:** Knead dough on a floured surface for 8-10 minutes, until smooth. Place in a lightly oiled bowl, cover, and let rise in a warm place for 1 hour or until doubled in size.
3. **Shape and Bake:** Punch down dough and shape into a loaf. Place in a greased loaf pan and let rise for another 30 minutes. Preheat oven to 375°F (190°C). Bake for 30-35 minutes, or until golden brown and the bread sounds hollow when tapped. Cool on a wire rack.

Greek Yogurt Honey Bread

Ingredients:

- 2 1/2 cups all-purpose flour
- 1/2 cup Greek yogurt
- 1/4 cup honey
- 1 packet (2 1/4 tsp) active dry yeast
- 1 cup warm water
- 2 tbsp olive oil
- 1/2 tsp salt

Instructions:

1. **Prepare Dough:** In a small bowl, dissolve yeast in warm water and let sit for 5 minutes until frothy. In a large bowl, combine flour and salt. Stir in yeast mixture, Greek yogurt, and olive oil until a dough forms.
2. **Knead and Rise:** Knead dough on a floured surface for 8-10 minutes, until smooth. Place in a lightly oiled bowl, cover, and let rise in a warm place for 1 hour or until doubled in size.
3. **Shape and Bake:** Punch down dough and shape into a loaf. Place in a greased loaf pan and let rise for another 30 minutes. Preheat oven to 375°F (190°C). Bake for 30-35 minutes, or until golden brown and the bread sounds hollow when tapped. Cool on a wire rack.

Potato Bread

Ingredients:

- 1 cup mashed potatoes (without butter or milk)
- 1 cup warm water
- 1/4 cup sugar
- 2 1/4 tsp active dry yeast (1 packet)
- 1/4 cup vegetable oil
- 1 egg
- 3 1/2 cups all-purpose flour
- 1 tsp salt

Instructions:

1. **Prepare Dough:** In a small bowl, dissolve yeast and sugar in warm water. Let sit for 5 minutes until frothy. In a large bowl, mix flour and salt. Add mashed potatoes, yeast mixture, oil, and egg. Stir until a dough forms.

2. **Knead and Rise:** Knead dough on a floured surface for about 10 minutes, until smooth. Place in a lightly oiled bowl, cover, and let rise in a warm place for about 1 hour, or until doubled in size.
3. **Shape and Bake:** Punch down dough and shape into a loaf. Place in a greased loaf pan and let rise for another 30 minutes. Preheat oven to 375°F (190°C). Bake for 35-40 minutes, or until golden brown and the bread sounds hollow when tapped. Cool on a wire rack.

Maple Oatmeal Bread

Ingredients:

- 1 cup old-fashioned oats
- 1 1/2 cups warm water
- 1/4 cup maple syrup
- 2 1/4 tsp active dry yeast (1 packet)
- 1/4 cup butter, softened
- 2 cups whole wheat flour
- 1 1/2 cups all-purpose flour
- 1 tsp salt

Instructions:

1. **Prepare Dough:** In a small bowl, dissolve yeast in warm water. Let sit for 5 minutes. In a large bowl, combine oats and maple syrup. Stir in yeast mixture and butter. Add whole wheat flour and salt, mixing well. Gradually add all-purpose flour until a dough forms.
2. **Knead and Rise:** Knead dough on a floured surface for about 8-10 minutes. Place in a lightly oiled bowl, cover, and let rise in a warm place for about 1 hour, or until doubled in size.
3. **Shape and Bake:** Punch down dough and shape into a loaf. Place in a greased loaf pan and let rise for another 30 minutes. Preheat oven to 375°F (190°C). Bake for 35-40 minutes, or until golden brown and a toothpick inserted into the center comes out clean. Cool on a wire rack.

Cranberry Walnut Bread

Ingredients:

- 3 cups all-purpose flour
- 1/2 cup sugar

- 1 packet (2 1/4 tsp) active dry yeast
- 1/2 tsp salt
- 1/2 cup chopped walnuts
- 1 cup dried cranberries
- 1 cup warm water
- 1/4 cup vegetable oil
- 1 egg

Instructions:

1. **Prepare Dough:** In a small bowl, dissolve yeast in warm water and let sit for 5 minutes. In a large bowl, mix flour, sugar, and salt. Add yeast mixture, oil, and egg. Stir until a dough forms. Fold in walnuts and cranberries.
2. **Knead and Rise:** Knead dough on a floured surface for about 10 minutes. Place in a lightly oiled bowl, cover, and let rise in a warm place for about 1 hour, or until doubled in size.
3. **Shape and Bake:** Punch down dough and shape into a loaf. Place in a greased loaf pan and let rise for another 30 minutes. Preheat oven to 375°F (190°C). Bake for 35-40 minutes, or until golden brown and the bread sounds hollow when tapped. Cool on a wire rack.

Country Rye Bread

Ingredients:

- 1 cup rye flour
- 2 cups all-purpose flour
- 1 packet (2 1/4 tsp) active dry yeast
- 1 1/2 cups warm water
- 1 tbsp caraway seeds
- 1 tbsp sugar
- 1 tsp salt
- 2 tbsp vegetable oil

Instructions:

1. **Prepare Dough:** In a small bowl, dissolve yeast and sugar in warm water and let sit for 5 minutes. In a large bowl, mix rye flour, all-purpose flour, and salt. Stir in yeast mixture and vegetable oil until a dough forms.

2. **Knead and Rise:** Knead dough on a floured surface for about 10 minutes, until smooth. Place in a lightly oiled bowl, cover, and let rise in a warm place for about 1 hour, or until doubled in size.
3. **Shape and Bake:** Punch down dough and shape into a loaf. Place in a greased loaf pan, sprinkle with caraway seeds, and let rise for another 30 minutes. Preheat oven to 375°F (190°C). Bake for 35-40 minutes, or until golden brown and the bread sounds hollow when tapped. Cool on a wire rack.

Fig and Walnut Bread

Ingredients:

- 3 cups all-purpose flour
- 1/2 cup sugar
- 1 packet (2 1/4 tsp) active dry yeast
- 1/2 tsp salt
- 1/2 cup chopped walnuts
- 1 cup dried figs, chopped
- 1 cup warm water
- 1/4 cup olive oil
- 1 egg

Instructions:

1. **Prepare Dough:** In a small bowl, dissolve yeast in warm water and let sit for 5 minutes. In a large bowl, mix flour, sugar, and salt. Add yeast mixture, olive oil, and egg. Stir until a dough forms. Fold in walnuts and figs.
2. **Knead and Rise:** Knead dough on a floured surface for about 10 minutes. Place in a lightly oiled bowl, cover, and let rise in a warm place for about 1 hour, or until doubled in size.
3. **Shape and Bake:** Punch down dough and shape into a loaf. Place in a greased loaf pan and let rise for another 30 minutes. Preheat oven to 375°F (190°C). Bake for 35-40 minutes, or until golden brown and a toothpick inserted into the center comes out clean. Cool on a wire rack.

Soft Pretzels

Ingredients:

- 1 1/2 cups warm water
- 1 packet (2 1/4 tsp) active dry yeast

- 1/4 cup granulated sugar
- 4 cups all-purpose flour
- 1 tsp salt
- 1/4 cup baking soda
- 1 egg, beaten
- Coarse salt, for sprinkling

Instructions:

1. **Prepare Dough:** In a small bowl, dissolve yeast and sugar in warm water and let sit for 5 minutes. In a large bowl, mix flour and salt. Add yeast mixture and stir until a dough forms.
2. **Knead and Rise:** Knead dough on a floured surface for about 8 minutes, until smooth. Place in a lightly oiled bowl, cover, and let rise in a warm place for about 1 hour, or until doubled in size.
3. **Shape Pretzels:** Preheat oven to 425°F (220°C). In a large pot, bring 4 cups of water and baking soda to a boil. Punch down dough and divide into 8 pieces. Roll each piece into a rope and shape into pretzels. Boil pretzels in the baking soda water for 30 seconds, then remove with a slotted spoon and place on a baking sheet. Brush with beaten egg and sprinkle with coarse salt.
4. **Bake:** Bake for 12-15 minutes, or until golden brown. Cool on a wire rack.

Asiago Cheese Bread

Ingredients:

- 1 cup warm water
- 1 packet (2 1/4 tsp) active dry yeast
- 1 tbsp sugar
- 3 cups all-purpose flour
- 1 1/2 cups grated Asiago cheese
- 1/4 cup olive oil
- 1 tsp salt
- 1/2 tsp garlic powder

Instructions:

1. **Prepare Dough:** In a small bowl, dissolve yeast and sugar in warm water. Let sit for 5 minutes until frothy. In a large bowl, mix flour and salt. Add yeast mixture, olive oil, and garlic powder. Stir until a dough forms. Fold in Asiago cheese.

2. **Knead and Rise:** Knead dough on a floured surface for about 8 minutes. Place in a lightly oiled bowl, cover, and let rise in a warm place for about 1 hour, or until doubled in size.
3. **Shape and Bake:** Punch down dough and shape into a loaf. Place in a greased loaf pan and let rise for another 30 minutes. Preheat oven to 375°F (190°C). Bake for 30-35 minutes, or until golden brown and the bread sounds hollow when tapped. Cool on a wire rack.

Muesli Bread

Ingredients:

- 1 cup muesli
- 1 1/2 cups warm milk
- 1 packet (2 1/4 tsp) active dry yeast
- 1/4 cup honey
- 3 cups whole wheat flour
- 1 cup all-purpose flour
- 1/4 cup vegetable oil
- 1 tsp salt

Instructions:

1. **Prepare Dough:** In a small bowl, dissolve yeast and honey in warm milk. Let sit for 5 minutes until frothy. In a large bowl, combine muesli, whole wheat flour,

all-purpose flour, and salt. Add yeast mixture and vegetable oil. Stir until a dough forms.
2. **Knead and Rise:** Knead dough on a floured surface for about 10 minutes. Place in a lightly oiled bowl, cover, and let rise in a warm place for about 1 hour, or until doubled in size.
3. **Shape and Bake:** Punch down dough and shape into a loaf. Place in a greased loaf pan and let rise for another 30 minutes. Preheat oven to 375°F (190°C). Bake for 35-40 minutes, or until golden brown and a toothpick inserted into the center comes out clean. Cool on a wire rack.

Apple Cheddar Bread

Ingredients:

- 1 cup shredded cheddar cheese
- 1 cup diced apples
- 1 1/2 cups warm milk
- 1 packet (2 1/4 tsp) active dry yeast
- 1/4 cup sugar
- 3 cups all-purpose flour
- 1/4 cup butter, softened
- 1 tsp salt

Instructions:

1. **Prepare Dough:** In a small bowl, dissolve yeast and sugar in warm milk. Let sit for 5 minutes until frothy. In a large bowl, mix flour and salt. Add yeast mixture and butter. Stir until a dough forms. Fold in cheddar cheese and diced apples.
2. **Knead and Rise:** Knead dough on a floured surface for about 8 minutes. Place in a lightly oiled bowl, cover, and let rise in a warm place for about 1 hour, or until doubled in size.
3. **Shape and Bake:** Punch down dough and shape into a loaf. Place in a greased loaf pan and let rise for another 30 minutes. Preheat oven to 375°F (190°C). Bake for 35-40 minutes, or until golden brown and the bread sounds hollow when tapped. Cool on a wire rack.

Sweet Cornbread

Ingredients:

- 1 cup cornmeal
- 1 cup all-purpose flour
- 1/4 cup sugar
- 1 tbsp baking powder
- 1/2 tsp salt
- 1 cup milk
- 1/4 cup melted butter
- 2 eggs

Instructions:

1. **Prepare Batter:** Preheat oven to 400°F (200°C). In a large bowl, combine cornmeal, flour, sugar, baking powder, and salt. In another bowl, whisk together milk, melted butter, and eggs. Add wet ingredients to dry ingredients and stir until just combined.
2. **Bake:** Pour batter into a greased 9-inch square baking pan or skillet. Bake for 20-25 minutes, or until golden brown and a toothpick inserted into the center comes out clean. Cool in the pan for a few minutes before cutting into squares.

Coconut Flour Bread

Ingredients:

- 1 cup coconut flour
- 1/2 cup almond flour
- 1/2 tsp baking powder
- 1/4 tsp salt
- 6 large eggs
- 1/4 cup coconut oil, melted
- 1 tbsp honey

Instructions:

1. **Prepare Batter:** Preheat oven to 350°F (175°C). In a large bowl, mix coconut flour, almond flour, baking powder, and salt. In another bowl, whisk together eggs, melted coconut oil, and honey. Add wet ingredients to dry ingredients and stir until smooth.
2. **Bake:** Pour batter into a greased 9x5-inch loaf pan. Bake for 30-35 minutes, or until golden brown and a toothpick inserted into the center comes out clean. Cool on a wire rack.

Herb and Cheese Scones

Ingredients:

- 2 cups all-purpose flour
- 1/4 cup grated Parmesan cheese
- 1 tbsp baking powder
- 1/2 tsp salt
- 1/2 tsp black pepper
- 1/2 cup cold butter, cut into cubes
- 1/2 cup shredded cheddar cheese
- 1/4 cup chopped fresh herbs (such as chives, parsley, or thyme)

- 3/4 cup milk

Instructions:

1. **Prepare Dough:** Preheat oven to 425°F (220°C). In a large bowl, mix flour, Parmesan cheese, baking powder, salt, and pepper. Cut in butter with a pastry cutter or fork until the mixture resembles coarse crumbs. Stir in cheddar cheese and herbs.
2. **Shape and Bake:** Add milk and stir until just combined. Turn dough out onto a floured surface and gently knead a few times. Roll out to 1-inch thickness and cut into triangles or rounds. Place on a baking sheet and bake for 12-15 minutes, or until golden brown. Cool on a wire rack.

Stuffed Garlic Bread

Ingredients:

- 1 loaf French or Italian bread
- 1/2 cup unsalted butter, softened
- 3 cloves garlic, minced
- 1/4 cup chopped fresh parsley
- 1 cup shredded mozzarella cheese
- 1/2 cup grated Parmesan cheese

Instructions:

1. **Prepare Filling:** Preheat oven to 375°F (190°C). In a bowl, mix softened butter, minced garlic, and chopped parsley.
2. **Prepare Bread:** Slice the loaf in half lengthwise. Spread the garlic butter mixture evenly on the cut sides of the bread. Sprinkle with mozzarella and Parmesan cheese.
3. **Bake:** Place bread on a baking sheet and bake for 10-12 minutes, or until cheese is melted and bubbly. For a crispy top, place under the broiler for an additional 1-2 minutes. Cut into slices and serve warm.

www.ingramcontent.com/pod-product-compliance
Lightning Source LLC
LaVergne TN
LVHW061958070526
838199LV00060B/4183